I WAS A SLAVE IN AMERICA UNTIL 2009

LILMA McLEAN SAMPLE

LitPrime Solutions
21250 Hawthorne Blvd
Suite 500, Torrance, CA 90503
www.litprime.com
Phone: 1-800-981-9893

© 2024 Lilma Mclean Sample. All rights reserved.

No part of this book may be reproduced, stored in a retrieval system, or transmitted by any means without the written permission of the author.

Published by LitPrime Solutions: 02/29/2024

ISBN: 979-8-88703-345-7(sc)
ISBN: 979-8-88703-346-4(e)

Any people depicted in stock imagery provided by iStock are models, and such images are being used for illustrative purposes only.

Certain stock imagery © iStock.

Because of the dynamic nature of the Internet, any web addresses or links contained in this book may have changed since publication and may no longer be valid. The views expressed in this work are solely those of the author and do not necessarily reflect the views of the publisher, and the publisher hereby disclaims any responsibility for them.

CONTENTS

I WAS A SLAVE IN AMERICA UNTIL 2009 1
WORKS CITED 49

I WAS A SLAVE IN AMERICA UNTIL 2009

When the black people was shackled in their homeland Africa and brought here to this country America history was written. Each one probably had families of their own. "After they were forced here from their country they were in a state of shock and horrifying fear." It was entirely a different situation than in their country.

In 1517 the Trans Atlantic slave trade officially began. "During the seventeenth and eighteenth century, the demand for slaves was at its peak. European slave traders quickly provided the labor…" The slave traders would not have been so successfully without the help of Africans. Africans provided them with other Africans to be enslaved.

When parents left their homes, went out to work or just being out, children were kidnapped from their homes. Many adults were kidnapped from the villages also. Africans kidnapped their own people. They were to be brought to a slave factory on the west coast of Africa.

In return, the slave traders gave the African kidnappers guns, textile, iron and other products.

"The captured Africans could spend as little as a few weeks and up to a year in a factory..." The estimation of slaves was twenty million and half did not make it to the coast. Numerous of the Africans died on the way before they reached the factory: the point where they were to be taken aboard ships bound for this new country. On one voyage, a ship of thirty crewmen and almost three hundred slave men, women and children took at least six weeks to come from Africa to the Americas.

The trip was long and horrible. Each slave had their ankle shackled to another slave. Their sleeping area was on hard un-sanded plank floors with only eighteen inches or less of head space. Because they were shackled to each other, there was no comfort or space for them to move about. It was difficult to change positions and standing was impossible. They were without light or air. The journey was long: this caused diseases to be contracted.

The slaves were kept below the deck before and during bad weather. Crewmen would then come to check on them after a storm has passed over. There they would find dead slaves entangled with slaves that are alive. Many died aboard the ship on their way to this country. Many jumped overboard the ship before they would submit to being enslaved.

Some slaves refused to eat but the crewmen forced food into them. Punishment was a way to make them eat also. Crewmen were very careful in the way that they would handle the slaves because they were thought of as property. They had to be in good health when they arrived in this country. Ten to twenty percent died aboard the ships. All were forced to make the journey. Traveling conditions were atrocious aboard the ship.

Kidnapped from their country, Africans left: fathers, mothers, sisters, brothers and children. After they arrived and set foot on American soil they had to be examined to see their conditions. Their eyes were checked for blindness, their teeth were checked to see if they were healthy. They were also checked for any mental or physical conditions. Even one slave buyer tasted a slave's sweat to check if the slave was healthy. Their entire body was examined before they were cast directly into slavery.

Time had begun to move on. It became a reality that this was actually happening to them. The slaves did not have any defense. Where were they to go? Who would help them? There was no place or way for them escaping. They were in the depth of slavery in this country, indeed.

Peter Wood Professor of History Duke University stated: "What do you think some of the issues are that contribute to shift from indentured

servitude to lifelong slavery? One of the things that go into that, I think the absence of feedback within the transatlantic slave system. For the Europeans who came to the new world, they had constant feedback to the old world: they could send letters, they could return home. The reputation of a given colony like Virginia or South Carolina or New York could be established and was something that was known about. For the African, the situation is completely different. If I'm an African brought to Virginia, brutally mistreated, there's no way that that negative feedback can return home to alert my relatives of the problem. And that lack of communication means that the exploitation can continue…"

The exploitation did go on throughout slavery's history of the black people. It was like an iron wall in America for those Africans. Anyone ought to be able to comprehend what it was like for the families. Only they suddenly disappeared and no knowledge of their whereabouts or if they were ever to be seen again. Likewise, the enslaved Africans was in the same world of dismays. As if they had sailed through a twilight zone to no return. There was no one to get in touch within the state of America or from their home land. The subjugation of every black person had an overwhelming broken heart.

Any black person or Caucasian that will say that the black slaves of centuries past did not have a broken heart is sadly erroneous. Those

Africans were human beings; they had a heart and human emotions. They loved just as well as any human that has a heart. The African slaves in the past endured long suffering. This is why the Caucasians looked toward Africa for their labor. The Caucasians knew that African labor was strong. The only way that the Africans endured the inhumane conditions that they were in was that there was not another way for them to choose a better and perfect way. African people found themselves in a lifelong servitude and their generation after generation being in the same situation.

The Caucasians ate the food that was prepared by the slaves. Their laundry was done by them. The Caucasians did not have a school for the slaves to attend teaching these trades pertaining to all that fell under the category of slave hood—hard labor. All this comprehension came natural with the slaves. Africans were a people of knowledge they were not ignorant, heathens, or animals as the Caucasians proclaimed them to be.

If the slaves even thought, the slave master's whip will become wet with their blood or even kill them. In due time, the slaves grew accustomed to it. They did not want to accept it though. "Slavery was primarily in the South, where existed in many different forms. Africans were enslaved on small farms, plantations, in cities and towns, inside homes, out in the fields and in industry and transportation…"

"By the middle of the eighteenth century, large numbers of fugitive slaves were risking punishment and even death in search of freedom. South Carolina's 1740 slaves code made it legal to kill a slave who was found away from the house or plantation, even if that person did not resist. Georgia's 1775 statutes, patterned after South Carolina's, actually encourages the killing of adult male runaways… the reward for returning a dead male slave was twice the amount offered for returning a live woman or child…"

There were numerous types of labor the black slaves had to do. Some of the house slaves were treated differently than the field slaves. Though both the two types of slaves' condition were unfair, the field slave's condition was a little worse that it should not have been mentioned. The current situation was a continuation with each slave: father, mother, sister and brother. Black slaves lived in a constant fear of being sold.

Families were separated then taken to the auction block and sold. Many of the slaves never saw their families again. Many were sold for punishment. Friends that the slaves made acquaintance with were taken to the auction blocks in various locations. They were never seen again neither.

Piece Butler ". . . Pierce, however, fell further and further into economic ruins, as he squandered away his vast fortune in gambling

and stock market speculation. In eighteen fifty-six his situation became so severe that the management of his finances was handed over to the trustees. To satisfy his enormous debt, they began by selling the Philadelphia mansion and liquidation other properties, but this was not enough. The trustees turned their attention to the property in Georgia, which consisted mostly of human slaves. In February eighteen fifty-nine the men traveled to Georgia to appraised Pierce Butler's share of slaves. Each person was examined and his or her value assessed. This was the preparation for what would be the largest single sale of human beings in United States history. It was an event that would come to be known as "the weeping time…"

"In March of eighteen eighty seven, the largest sale of human beings in the history in the United States took place at a racetrack in Savannah, Georgia. During the two days of the sale, raindrops fell unceasingly on the racetrack. It was almost as though the heavens were crying. So, two fell teardrops from many of the four hundred and thirty six men, women, and children who were auctioned off during the two days. The sale would therefore be known as "the weeping time…"

There were times that the black men and women disagreed with each other. They cherished the love that they had despite their conditions, which was inhumane. It plainly can be known by the history that is

recorded. The black women were bound with agony as they carrying their fetes. That beyond any doubt, the conditions they were in had a devastating impact on the women and the life of their fetes.

While the fetes are yet in the womb, it is being taught betrayal. The betrayal passed to generation to generation until finally it became heredity. The betrayal that the fetes inherit it was because of the dammed thing called slavery. Some told on the others to the slave masters. This was a way of survival from their master's whip. They had to submit to "all" conditions of the times.

The humiliation, discrimination and inhumanly treatment forced upon the black people here in America throughout centuries have been a terrible situation. African slaves as a whole loved each other before and after they arrived here to America. When years begun to pass into centuries of slavery; that love became a cool breeze blowing between them.

". . . Eric Foner Professor of History Columbia University said: "Now, in the South, southern insisted that slavery was absolutely essential to the story of progress. Without slavery, you could not have civilization, they said. Slavery freed the upper class from the need to do manual labor, to worry about economic day-to-day realities, and therefore gave them the time and the intellectual ability to devote

themselves to the arts and literature and mechanical advantages and inventions of all kinds. So that it was slavery itself which made the progress of civilization possible..."

This was absolutely one of the Caucasian slave owner's thoughts. Secondly, another thought of theirs was that the black slaves were "their" property. Thirdly, they thought that God had made them masters over black people. Their final thought was that the slaves were supposed to serve and obey them according to the Holy Scripture all the days of their lives. This is the scripture that the Caucasians was justifying themselves with Genesis chapter 9:24-27.

There are some Caucasians that are still based upon these Scriptures today. What did they think about Genesis chapter 27:37-40? Esau was Isaac blood son just as Jacob. These Scriptures even go as far as into the book of Joshua. Firstly, Caucasians were not and are not Jews.

How could any of those Caucasians think in the days of slavery? In which they were in control. That if slavery did not exist. There would not be a civilization. Civilization was in existence then. Slavery was so hideous and a filtration; something that seems unreal, but it was. It was just sifted on through.

Fredrick Douglas once said, ". . . I now understand what had been to me a most perplexing—to wit, the white man's power to enslave

the black man—from that moment, I understood the pathway from slavery to freedom."

Fredrick Douglas overheard his master Hugh Auld statement to his wife Sophia when he was ten years old at his master Hugh's home in Baltimore. Auld explained to his wife Sophia that:

". . . If you give a nigger an inch, he will take an ell. A nigger should know nothing but to obey his master—to do as told to do. Learning would spoil the best nigger in the world. "Now", said he "if you teach that nigger to read, there would be no keeping him. It would forever unfit him to be a slave. He would at once come unmanageable, and of no value to his master. As to himself, it could do him no good, but a great deal of harm. It would make him discontented and unhappy."

This is the statement that gave Frederick Douglas the mind to be free. He was so deeply hurt from the conversation. Frederick Douglas went on to tell of his life; the murders and hardships. He was then determined to be free. When he became older he escaped the slavery and became one of our black great leaders.

When the sixteenth president, Abraham Lincoln, first came into politics he made a statement. It was concerning black slaves in one of his debates. He explained that while he was not asking for equality, he believed that the colored people should get the rights granted in the

Declaration of Independence: life, liberty, and the pursuit of happiness. This statement that he made is grieving to my heart.

He was not for the black people. The Emancipation Proclamation did not free all slaves in the United States. It only freed slaves in states that were not in the union. Those states, which were supported of the union, he offered the slave-owners compensation if they would give up their slaves.

The states which were offered compensation refused his offer and kept their property as the slaves were called.

President Lincoln issued a degree stating if the rebellious states did not return to the union by a designated date, freedom will be granted to all slaves within those states. The President did not set the entirety of slaves free until he saw that he had to. These two reasons state why President Lincoln was not for the black slaves: Firstly, he said that he was not asking for equality for them. Secondly, after becoming President, he had the power to set all black slaves free. Instead, he made offers to the slave owners that if they give up their slaves he will give them compensation for them. When the owners of these slaves refused he threatens them. He threatened that if they did not return to the union he will set all black slaves free.

This was all about the politics for this sixteenth president. Just as

it has been with the entire political organizations throughout history. The Declaration of Independence states that all men are created equal. "The reason this document was brought forward is to say: when the Declaration of Independence was written, it was not for the blacks here in America. It was written for the Caucasians; the colonies. They were looking for freedom from under the British Crown."

The black people were not members of those colonies. They were not members of any political or social event. There was not anything intended for the black human race here in America—but slavery! Black people were not included in the Constitution of the United States of America when it was constituted. Slavery is a condition that will kill men's very strength of character. There is no will to live because slavery echoes extremely to the soul.

Dred Scott knew he was a human being and knew he was of importance. He knew also that he was black and he was a slave. This man, Dred Scott who the creator created along with all mankind did not give up. He and the slaves wanted to be free just as the Caucasians. From 1847 to1857 he battled in the courts until he was finally freed. He sued the state of St. Louise, Missouri, in which he lived for his freedom.

His case went even to the Supreme Court of the United States. The Supreme Court denied him his freedom because he was black and not

a citizen. In other words, he was not a Caucasian, nor did he have the rights of an American citizen. The Supreme Court did not free him nor did any court in the United States of America. His first slave master's sons freed him after many years of struggle. After his freedom, he only lived nine months.

You can see that he pressed on. He helped pave the way for the black race today and all that are in an oppressed captious conditions. During the entirety of slavery, black slaves knew that they were not free. The Caucasians made it very hard for the black people afterwards. They did not want to give up their slave-hood.

Many slaves were trying always to set themselves free from the Caucasians slavery. They came up with plots like Nat Turner which cannot be justified for his action. He was only trying to be free to his knowledge. Numerous others attempted to take over certain places and areas. But their plots were discovered there was no place for them to go or escape. They were hunted down like animals until they were caught and then hanged.

The Underground Railroad helped numerous black slaves to escape from slavery. ". . . By the early 19th century, the organization became so successful that it is estimated that between 1810 and 1850 100.000 slaves escaped from the South through the Underground Railroad…"

Some individuals may not know that this is an organization not a railroad track that trains travel on carrying passengers from place to place.

This Underground Railroad was a network consisting of people that had joined together a secret escape route for the escaping slaves. The organization was kept very secret because of the search parties and slave catchers. If the slaves were caught they were either killed or returned back to their masters.

Freed Africans and escaped slaves helped other fleeing slaves. One individual alone of the great slave fugitives was Harriet Tubman. After she escaped she returned to various slave states and helped numerous of time to lead the way for the escaping slaves. She would lead slaves on the route north and to Canada.

Lynching was still at its greatest. Hanging of the black men was nothing to the Caucasians. Taking the life of a black man was very common. Walking by the wayside, black men could be seen hanging in trees with the nose about their necks. Years later hanging of black men slowed down to an extent.

The black men knew not to cause disturbances in the Caucasian community. There were times if a black man took a Caucasian life he would be pursued until apprehended, put on trial then judgment would

be pronounced on him. The death sentence would be announced to him, or a very long incarceration that would be his life.

There were Caucasians that was opposed to the slavery condition. Honor to John Brown is due. John Brown, the Caucasian abolitionist, and his family. John Brown and his family continently fought with the slave-owners. It was in the hearts of this family to detest the damnable thing slavery.

They were opposed to it; insomuch that he and twenty one men raided the federal arsenal at Harpers Ferry. He wanted to arm the black slaves with the weapons. This was to try and create a war against slavery. Five blacks and sixteen Caucasians. These brave and courageous men stood with this honorable man John Brown on October 16, 1859. Some of those men that lost their lives in the raid at Harpers Ferry were John Browns own sons.

After he was wounded and captured at Harpers Ferry. They arrested him for treason.

"Lying on a cot in the court room. Before hearing his sentence, he was allowed to address the court. He said, I believe to have interfered as I have done,—in behalf of His despised poor, was not wrong, but right. Now if it be deem necessary that I should forfeit my life for the furtherance of the ends of justice, and mingle my blood further with

the blood of my children, and with the blood of millions in this slave country whose rights are disregarded by wicked, cruel, and unjust enactments, I summit so let it be done."

John brown and his men were not justified for their acts of violence. He did these things in his heart; hoping that slaves might be free one day. This Caucasian abolitionist and his men gave up their lives for the cause of slavery. Bravery and honor should still be due to John Brown and his men because of their actions at Harpers Ferry or any place else.

The Caucasians that was against slavery fought for blacks. The slaves' owners knew that their own kind was fighting them for keeping black human beings in slavery. Their own kind was fighting against them causing divisions amongst each other. Even this did not move in their hearts any compassion whatsoever concerning their ungodly unrighteousness that they had brought about. For those black people that they kidnapped did not have a human defense on their side.

Over the two hundred and fifty years of slavery, the black enslaved ancestors in America only had Christ. The degree, agony, and defeat in this serious hour. Life of black people was spitefully used as an animal life. The Caucasian race did have the Constitutional rights to all that was written in the Constitution until 2009. What happened in 2009? A new president has been elected.

The law that was passed in this country to carry concealed weapons states that one may carry a concealed weapon if there are no criminal or insanities backgrounds found. Society knew the Caucasians here in America the law had protected them from day one. Their communities, their lives, were safe-guarded at all times.

There was no need to pass this law. The law to carry concealed weapons was a mistake. It is passed now and it has gotten out of hand. What happened? When the law to carry these weapons was passed men possessed these weapons for evil. Weapons along with drugs and alcohol are doing a marvelous job here in America.

Drugs and alcohol did not have anything to do with the condition of the blacks in this country. The ancestors were forced into slavery here in America. They became a people without a name or country. They did not turn to drugs or alcohol. It is probably not known whether there were drugs at the time. Alcohol was prohibited during the time of slavery that our ancestors could indulge in. Their lives were filled with hardship though. There was not time. Their work days were on the rising of the sun until the going down of the same.

Even the women carrying their fetes work day was the same as the men. Up until it was the very moment for them to deliver their unborn that the day of labor came to an end. Females were given only

one month to recover after giving birth. They were put back at hard labor again. Carrying their newly born on their backs. There is no record in history of a drug or alcohol conditions amongst the slaves to my knowledge.

Drugs, alcohol and other sources is the major problem here in America today. Marce H. Morial, The Urban League's president said, "Empowering Black men to reach their full potential is the most serious economic and civil rights challenge we face today." Morial said, "Ensuring their future is critical, not just the African-American community, but for the prosperity, health and well-being of the entire American family…"

These weapons are causing the murder of each black male today. Black males carry the seed of this race. Every black male that is murdered is causing extinction of the black race. If the males become extinct that will be the end of black human beings. In cities where the policing are needed most has no protection from the violence of every day. In the black communities there are little or no policing.

This is one of the reasons crimes are so easily committed. Do any of you black men own an aircraft fleece, ship fleece, or even a freight fleece, which you may transport drugs, guns, into this country or from place to place? No! Blacks should lay the guns down against

each other. "Stop the violence". This murdering must come to an end. There are more murders at present than in the past since the gun law was passed.

If only the morals of black men and also females was built up, so that they would reach their full potential. They are so important. Christ loves them. If anybody abuses their lives, male or female, with these conditions drugs and alcohol this is enslaving one's self. If it is a problem, ask Christ to help. Remember He was there during the overwhelming days of the slavery.

Anything that causes the body and mind not to perform rationally is slavery; slavery of one's self. No one has forced the drugs and alcohol into anyone's bodies. They are causing the lost of everything that is dear. The family suffers most with ones negligence. Lost of life is devastating.

Diverse people have allowed these conditions, "which does not have a color limit" to approach and take over throughout the entire world. Life has not been a bed of roses. It has not been for the black male or the female. The Lord did not say that it would be.

America is congested at this point with all forms of drugs and alcohol. They do absorb the human brain. They cause all kinds of breakdown in the body. This is pertaining to all that have and will abuse themselves with these conditions. Slavery, discrimination and

hardship do not give anyone the right to abuse him or her life. Turning to drugs and alcohol is no way out or an excuse.

Sweat and blood have been given to this country by the black people. Blacks are free. We must refrain from anything that will cause the brain to respond to negativity. There is no slavery of the Caucasians today. There are not anymore "Uncle Toms" to tell to the slave masters. The Black Codes and the Jim Crow laws are gone forever.

Bringing Hip-Hop and the Music Industry into focus here. In their lyrics, that are used, rappers claimed they are sending a message to the black people concerning their condition. It cannot be seen where a message is being sent. Their foul music and lyrics did not have any reflection at all on the suffering and the agony black people suffered when they were enslaved by the Caucasian race.

The Hip-Hop industry knew in the beginning when the first recordings were put on the market that our black children was listening and learning its slime. It has been years of these distasteful lyrics in rapping that have lead to the disrespect of black women. Disrespect to sex and to the black race.

"Now that slavery here in America is over what will their lyrics cry out today?" Russell Simmons, the Chairman of the Hip-Hop Summit Action Network (HSAN), held a meeting speaking of the concerns of

the lyrics that is being used in Hip-Hop and who they target—females. HSAN is a non-profit, non-partisan national coalition of Hip-Hop artists' entertainment industry leaders. They believe that Hip-Hop is an enormously influential agent for social change, which must be responsibly utilized to fight the war on poverty and injustice.

Mister Simmons stated in an exclusive interview for The Sunday Tribune on the twenty second of April, 2007 he said, "For me, anytime we discuss race, sexism and misogyny it's good. What we don't want to do is be like the previous generation and sweep it under the rug."

The previous generation did not sweep anything under the rug as mister Simmons stated. Counting from one generation, or two, up until Mister Simmons made his interview with the Sunday Tribune. The black neighborhood was not congested with guns, drugs and alcohol as they are today. They can teach on how to count your money, do not get a credit card, black power—or whatever they are trying to teach.

Blacks are not going to think of themselves as being nobody anymore. They must think of their selves highly than they did during the slavery days. Hell with its fury was turned loose onto the black people. It is the dawning of a new day. Living in the present now, if God is willing will look for the further. If slavery exists today it is because there are blacks secretly being held.

Everyone is free to do evil and to be corrupted. If enslaved by another human being or any kind of a captive conditions. This is far from being liberated; "free". It is not right to live in any kind of slavery. Not being equal and enslaved is a sin. It is worst than a contagious decease that cannot be healed. There is no cure for it only to be set free.

I was a slave here in American until the year 2009. I am free now along with all black Americans. I am not a colored person, a nigger, or African-American. I refuse to acknowledge these phrases. These phrases are proving that the black people still does not have any part in this country America. I am a black American woman; a human being.

I could not help but to recall my life's history. My thoughts went out into my history I cannot compare the slavery of the black people centuries ago by the slavery that I had. As I grew older I could not see where slavery had ended. My slavery was not centuries ago. The agony and the hurt that is associated with my life is a different time than the old slaves. Although, I my sister and my friend. We were terrified to walk the roads during the day and by night. We were terrified at all times: fearful of being kidnapped or murdered. Every evil come upon us by the Caucasian males.

It has been known numerous of time that the female Caucasians took part in the rot to instigate it. I was permitted to attend school where

there was inadequate food, clothing and shelter. All but the right things; insufficiency was the bottom line. I left my home town in the South. I came north figuring that things would be different. It was not. I was still called a nigger by Caucasians as I walked on my block in the city.

Black people and Caucasian people are foreigners in this land America. History records both races came from a different country. The Caucasians are not called European Caucasians. No, they are called American Caucasians and they cannot truthfully declare this land is theirs only. Through sweat and hard toiling of the black man this great country was built. The Caucasians and the blacks are here. Blacks and Caucasians are going to live in this country collectively.

The previous generations of slave's centuries past would be delighted to have seen the year 2009. Previously, this black man put in his bid for presidency and become a candidate to be President of this country was just wonderful. To embrace this great thing that the Lord has done for the black people here in America is good. The creator intervened here.

This America is a beautiful land and country. Decades ago, it was assumed by some black leaders that black people should go back to Africa. No blacks at that time had to go back to Africa. Black Americans does not have to go today. Know that for the duration of over two hundred years the black race were enslaved and oppressed by

the Caucasians in America. You are not enslaved any longer get together black people and be delighted.

This country is the black people's home today. America is their country. Africa is not their country. Black people are descendents. The Lord looked upon the oppression of the Israelites in the land of Egypt. Know for a surety, Christ has looked upon the oppression of the black people here in America. The Israelites were enslaved by the Egyptians for over four hundred years. The Lord ordains Moses as His leader to lead the Israelites out of slavery in the land of Egypt. Furthermore this is what was about to be told to you in regarding the new President.

Jesus Christ did not overlook the affliction of the black people. Centuries had conceded that slavery still abounded in this country. That did not give any indication that Christ forgot the slavery of the black people. Christ ordains Barack Obama to go through the channels of education. He obtains knowledge to achieve this office as President of the United States of America. One nation under God, giving him compassion and favor for all nationality, race, creed and color.

Cry aloud with tears and great joy. Give thanks to your creator God Almighty, Jesus Christ. He has set the blacks free through Barack Obama. He is the first black man ever to become President of the United

States of America. He was sworn into office as President of the United States of America in the year 2009.

Barack Obama is the first black man to attain this honor ever. This is President of this United States of America. This is what has set the black people free today. Freedom was a long time coming. Freedom is here to stay. America is not striving to reach freedom and equality anymore. When this black man Barack Obama became President of the United States, this is what has made the black race free and equal with the Caucasian race

Please black people, do not ever presume that any assemblage of people otherwise any organizations have placed this black man in immense honor and authority. Head of State, Commander and Chief, it is the maximum honor that one can achieve here in America. This was the work of Christ.

This should not have come to be such astonishment to you black people. The Lord did bring an amazing new election of this year 2009. He did do marvelously and put this black man in power to lead this vast and powerful nation. Slavery should never have been in this United States of America.

It should not have prevailed on the Lords entire Earth. Slavery has been worldwide for centuries amongst different nations. Black citizens

have been set unconventional free of bondage which was so obviously seen. Bestow all the honor and praise up to God. He "did not" forget your afflictions. Your daily existence was slavery.

Black people at this time have to repent. You have not forgiven the Caucasians for the inhumanity and the ungodly conditions in which they forced upon you. Christ wants absolution through you for them. It was their greed and lust and it cannot be said of their ignorance.

There was no ending of the desolation as long as the slavery condition was at hand. The black people were considered as animals. Not any longer. An animal cannot convert to a human being and become the head of a nation. Africa was the black ancestor's home and country centuries past. America is the home and country of blacks the same as it is for the Caucasians.

This editorial column was recently found on the Internet, "France to compensate nuclear test victims. PARIS-The French government offered for the first time Tuesday to compensate victims of nuclear test in Algeria and South Pacific, bowing to decades of pressure by people sicken by radiation-and seeking to sooth France's conscience." "It's time for our country to be at peace with itself, at peace thanks to a system of compensation and reparation." French Defense Minister, Herve Morin, said in presenting a draft law on the payouts.

Compensation should be given to the black people here in America today on behalf of the slavery that they underwent. The past two hundred fifty years that the blacks were in slavery sent an era of despair, defeat, abuse and fatality cascading right through the souls of the black people here in this United States of America. Not including the Holocaust. Not other peoples. The black people who were enslaved in this country for centuries—not decades ago.

How can the Africkan World Repatriation and Reparation Truth Commission (AWRRTC) Doctor Harmet Maulana, the Commission's Co-Chairman, ask for compensation for Africa? The slavery took place here in America with blacks. Not in Africa. Black Americans have long left the ancestral breed of African life. They have made their own culture and have become a new people: Black Americans.

What happened with the Trans-Atlantic slave trade? Africans sold their own kind to the traders for guns, iron and additional products. It was not Doctor Hamet Maulana, not mordant day Africa, but the Africans that did this they were his ancestors. Also, what damage did the Trans-Atlantic slave trade do to Africa the country?

Black Americans that were enslaved here in this country over two centuries ago their descendants are here in this country America today. They are who supposed to be compensated for that unholy, unrighteous

and hideous condition of slavery that was forced upon them and their ancestors past. No organizations of any kind suppose to be included. Black Americans individuals were slaves up until 2009, and was victims of Africa and of America.

Just until recently the blacks was able by the help of Christ to come out of that bondage. You are looking at approximately over two centuries of slavery. Hell on Earth for innocent black people. This situation that came from greed, exploitation, murder and power was committed by the Caucasians within the entire black race of people here in America not in Africa.

This issue regarding America apologizing does not have anything to do with that era of bondage. Otherwise, America took from the black people that it could not give back: life, respect, honor and peace. These are just a few. The entirety of slavery within this country did cause an overwhelming dark cloud. Also, there is another website of curiosity on the Internet.

It is called Project 21 the National Leadership Network of Black Conservatives. This is written on one of the websites. "America has apologized," By Mychal Massie. Mychal said, "The United States didn't invent slavery. While it is historical fact that certain regions participated in and benefited from slavery, it should also be pointed out

that America had the good sense to eliminate slavery and emancipate its slaves—acknowledging their full rights and citizenship…"

Mychal speaks of blacks that are holding different powerful positions here in America. He also spoke of black billionaires such as Opera Winfrey and others. These people have worked hard and long for what they have. America did not give them anything; they got it for themselves. Who is he trying to convince how America has taken care of the black people? He mentions that people come to the United States to start a new life. That is true. The people that come seeking a change of life really get it. They are well taken care of. Better than the native black Americans are.

Mychal also said, "I grow weary of the repetitious mantra of how bad blacks have had it or have it now. Not everyone came here in chains, Africans included. But people still come here to escape bondage and start in a new life, Africans included…"

Wonder where he got his information from. It is good to have come across his website. Currently, what are individuals thoughts concerning the centuries of slavery that blacks have encounter were force into? Who actually care to know? Does anyone really care to know the depth of slavery? Black history was not properly taught in the public schools in America. The public schools taught about the Civil Rights movement of nineteenth fifty.

Mychal's race, creed or nationality was not mentioned on the website. He should go back and read black history again. Maybe he will not get weary of what happened to the blacks here in the United States of America. The hard times that the blacks had half of black Americans never have read it. There are blacks that did not get much schooling. A great number has not had any schooling at all. Therefore, many black people have never heard of black history or black history month.

This gives one that has not heard of black history a little knowledge. The teaching of black history month does not go into the dept but it helps. If all the inhumane heartless conditions were really exposed in the schools someone could be very angry. Reading Mychal's article was very disturbing.

It seems that he have read the black slave history. Yet it does not appear to have given him the understanding of the suffering of these people that did not cause the terrible and horrible slavery that was forced upon them. Those ships were waiting there on the west coast of Africa.

The crews waited to pack as many aboard ships as possible at the command of their captains. Then again wonder if Mychal is apologizing for America. Or is he one that has never lived a second in slavery. There is a possible chance of him really not knowing. Until the time passes

that everyone recognize that we are free and equal human beings there are going to be every kind of negativity.

Weigh it out on a scale of justice. There was not any mercy or faith. Hatred for the blacks in the hearts of the Caucasians condoned that act of injustice. Can it ever be comprehend? How can the Caucasians hate with a great passion for black people?

There might be some that will say that is not true. But it has got to go along with the phrase… "Action speaks louder than words". The blacks freed themselves from that unholy condition. When blacks reached out and caused society to be disturbed. They were trying to get what belonged to them. All that has been accomplished the black people did it. Those were shameful days of slavery; a time there in history.

"On March 3, 1865, Congress established the Bureau of Refugees, Freemen, and Abandoned Lands, also known as the Freemen's Bureau. It was to function for only one year, but on July 16, 1866, Congress extended the life of the bureau over the veto of Presiding Andrew Jackson. The bureau was organized under the War Department with Major General Oliver O. Howard as the commissioner. The bureau's chief focus was to provide food, medical care, help with resettlement, administer justice; manage abandoned and confiscated property, regulate labor, and establish schools. Over 1,000 schools were built, teachers-

trained institutions were created, and several black colleges were founded and financed with the help of the bureau. Despite the bureau's success in education, it was unable to alleviate many problems, especially in regard to land management when the Bureau gave 850.000 acres of abandoned and confiscated land to Freemen, President Andrew Jackson returned the land to confederate owners. Without the resettlement of land, the bureau instead focused on helping Freemen gain work. They encouraged them to work on plantations, but this eventually led to oppressive share cropping and tenancy arrangement. The progressive goals of the bureau, however, were not enough to make up for inadequate funds that plaque its existence. In 1869, Congress terminated the entire bureau's work except for its efforts in education. In 1870, that two was ended."

"In March 1866, congress passed the Civil Rights Act. Although Jackson vetoed the bill, the unity of the Republican Party led to its passage. The legislation gave blacks the rights and privileges of full citizenship and the Black Codes were eliminated. Although most Black Codes were abolished, some states legislatures revised and implemented less severe codes."

Can you look at these two dates from 1865 to 1866? What America gave was soon taken back. 850.000 acres of land was given, schools were built, and some colleges were founded. Black people were given food and medical care. They were given help with settling in the abandoned and confiscated land that was given to the Freemen. As time pass even the education was abandoned because lack of funds.

"The black codes of 1865 prohibit the black people from entering towns and cities. Almost every aspect of life was regulated, including the freedom to roam. Many codes prohibited blacks from entering towns without permission. In Opelousas, Louisiana, blacks needed permission from their employer to enter the town, and that stated the nature and length of the visit was required. Any black found without a note after ten o'clock at night was subjected to imprisonment."

The Jim Crow law followed after the codes. Lands that the blacks had gotten were repossessed. Sharecropping were some of the conditions that blacks had to face. They needed tools, seeds, food, and clothing for themselves. These things were gotten on time. Blacks sometime were overdrawn at the end of the year as the Caucasians informed them.

They did not have anything to show for their labor: anything, but hard times of sorrow over and over. It was as if they were never freed by pen and paper. Codes that came about after slavery supposed to have ended. It kept blacks life in the same condition. Slavery just kept rolling on throughout history. Blacks were still house slaves and at hard labor.

Read the history of slavery. See that slavery did not end at this time. Read about sharecropping. At the end of the year there was nothing to look forward to. Most black share croppers had a deficit at the end of the year. There was nothing during the year only the little that there was that was edible. There was the lack of food. Working in the tobacco and cotton fields was not a day of fun and relaxing.

Black organizations that said that they were helping did the best that could be done. Congress passed the Civil Rights Act in 1866. The Legislation gave to black people privileges and "full" citizenship. Now the Civil Rights Act was passed on that date here. The NAACP (the advancement of colored people) organization has been here since 1909.

What did the NAACP black leaders in this organization do? The best that could be expected the extreme dislike for blacks; discontentment. Black people were giving full civil rights by Congress in 1866. Now this was also confiscated. For example, when the honorable Rosa Parks refused to give up her seat to the Caucasian male on a bus this is where it all began to really be seen. Showing that slavery of the black people had not ended in 1950 up until the year of 2009.

The article states:

"Rosa Parks was born February 4, 1913, in Tuskegee Alabama to James McCauley and Leona McCauley. On December 1, 1955 forty three year old Rosa boarded a Montgomery, Alabama city bus after finishing work as a tailor assistant at Montgomery fair department store. As all blacks patrons were required to do, she paid her fair at the front of the bus and then re-boarded in the rear. She sat in a vacant seat in the back next to a man and across the aisle from two women. After a few stops, the seats in the front of the bus became full, and a white man who had boarded stood in the aisle. The bus driver asked Parks, the man next to her, and the two women to let the white man have their seats. As the others moved, Parks remained in her seat. The bus driver again asked her to move, but she refused. The bus driver called the police, and she was arrested. She did not know it at the time, but this courageous act would lead to a 382 day bus boycott and the desegregation of buses throughout the United States."

There were similar cases but they did not go to the point that received national recognition. There are black people that created situations that have helped the conditions.

Were there anything else could be done? After this organization was established? Why was there still a fight to be fought? The black leaders fought with little as they had. The Civil Rights Movement of 1950 did not hardly accomplish anything either in that era. There was really a fight about it. Following, the schools and facilities were open to us. Why was there a fight for the rights that had been given to us over a century past?

There was discrimination in every channel. There was lost of life. It was kept on the front burner. Blacks have really held it fast and took full advantage of all with as little as they had. Looking at over a century here since the Civil Rights Act was declared, the legislation gave black people their "full" privileges and citizenship. The black leaders knew that they were still in slavery. It was not the full blown slavery as the former ancestors were in. It was still slavery. They have stayed on top of the in-bondage situation.

These black leaders and their organization did not, and could not, accomplish much. They have come a long way from yesterday. Then again they have made great progress here in this country concerning where the black people were fifty years ago. There is a black president today. Wonderful things are opening.

You might wonder why it is continuing to be explained the ending of slavery in the year 2009. Well this is the beginning of a new era. There is a black President. If the President had not have won the election of 2009 slavery would be present today. If the honorable Rosa Parks had given up her seat to the Caucasian there would not be a black President today.

Reverend Jessie Jackson made a statement. His statement appeared in the West Side Weekly newspaper in Philadelphia Pennsylvania. He made the statement in 2008. In addition he was in slavery at that time. He said, "Today, we are free, not equal." He added, "So you can't celebrate until the game is over". Being that he was enslaved at that time, he phrases his statement as he did because we were not free in 2008.

Reverend Al Sharpton, Reverend Jackson and the entirety of black leaders seems to be totally concerned about being called a name. It also seems to me that they are so concerned if one of another race call blacks the "N" word. They were very upset about the Caucasian using the "slanderous" words concerning a group of black females.

The "N" word as it is called it is fine. You can go on and forget about being called names or name-calling. "I am not speaking to African

American; colored people or niggers I am speaking to black American people." Believe it. You are called many of names. We black people call each other a nigger. Then get offended if one from another race calls you out of this phrase.

Which is important to you, would you rather be called a nigger with integrity, than called a nigger without integrity? Have you ever heard the old saying? "Sticks and stones may break my bones but words will never hurt me." If any blacks have heard this saying there is no doubt that they have not. They should take heed to it. This is a true and virtuous saying. Do not forget it.

Name-calling is not the issue. You are the issue here and not name calling. Black people were not even on the agenda until 2009… remember. The lack of knowledge is a devastating deficient. Different cultures denied the life that the creator gave to the black race. These leaders wanted to put an end to the discrimination. It is an overwhelming condition. How are they going to stop prejudice against blacks that has been for centuries? There will always be prejudice and racism in America. It is in the hearts of Caucasians: they will not let it go. They are afraid to. Their belief is that black peoples are slaves and always suppose to be to them.

Do unto others as you would have them do unto you. So, could that be the case? Do they think that black people will do the same unto them? That is imposing slavery upon the Caucasians as they did unto the blacks. This might be a freighting and devastating sensitivity with them.

This is why I will not dare to say the Caucasians did not know better. Slavery was adopted for the black people centuries ago in America by them. The Caucasians knew their plan from day one when the first Africans were kidnapped. They were taken to slave factories and held there in inhumane conditions. The Caucasians wanted the riches that came from America's soil. So, they enslaved the black people because they did not want to work for it themselves. This is what happened.

The worst scenario was after enslaving the blacks the treatment of them was worse than the enslavement. If there is any blacks that will go for their apology that is good. I suppose there are blacks who would rather, or prefer slavery than their freedom. Please do not misunderstand. Forgive the Caucasians and love them, but do not accept their apology.

They are not the only people that you have to love. We do not have hatred in our hearts for anyone. We are free and equal. No groups of people or organization give this to you. You have obtained these yourselves. So fret not black people. In biblical days, Aaron with his sister Marion brought about the first discrimination against blacks.

They were prejudice against Moses' black Ethiopian wife. Christ was not pleased with the discrimination then. He is definitely not pleased with it today.

Throughout history there has been a denial of these people. Denials bind up in one thing which is hate. The last thing is to be recognized. Do not worry about that either. You are black beautiful people. This is why you are denied. Black people woolly nappy hair is the sign of deity. Their black skin represents royalty.

Black women you do not have to wear the false hair to make yourselves attractive. You are beautiful just the way you are. Perms that are on the market are causing black women to lose their beautiful hair. Black women are losing their hair daily.

Meanwhile, this industrial organization is becoming very rich. Also, black men and women are very attractive. The men have got to understand that black women are standing by them. The women should not be called foul names as in the song. They should be treated with respect and the black men are suppose to receive the same due respect. They are partners; they came through slavery centuries ago and the latter day slavery together.

In the dept of slavery the black man was powerless. He saw the harassment of the black women. How they were flogged while carrying their unborn. How he was fastened to the ground and flogged himself. Most have read about the Caucasians slavery in this present day. The black man and women have got to stand together or fall. They must understand that their education is of most importance.

A few black people here in America were never educated. There are only a few which made it to a higher education in the past. Only they that were of a lighter complexion are ones with money. This is not a prejudice statement. This is the way that things happened in the past. Especially in southern states where the Codes and the Jim Crow laws were harsh.

Channels to higher education are open to the blackest of the black people today. Failing to be educated is a drastic mistake. It also is slavery to one's self here in this mordant day. No matter who is President of our country, we do not have any reason why that we cannot get the education. One will never overcome until the proper education is obtained.

Look at history and see for yourself. When anyone completes an education they are able to comprehend society and the law of the land: everything that is gotten within the law. We black people have the ability to triumph. The mind that God gave to one is more powerful than can be imaged. We have got to go out there and get the education.

You will see that your life will be even better. We have a defense today though. This is why education is the key that has unlocked those doors that was shut to us. Without an education here in America, we will stagger around as blind people begging society to give a helping hand "to the poor and needy." We can get it for ourselves—honestly.

Devoid of education for black people will be impossible to overcome. Over 98 years has passed since the NAACP organization came into action. Education is necessities not negativity. Get the education that you are supposed to have. It is not hard to do. There are free educational programs throughout every state. This state that I live in has free programs. If one is an adult there are free programs for you to gain your G.E.D. or diploma.

Here we are today. It is time for us to triumph over this particular heredity that slavery caused. We have to tuck it under our hats as another experience and go on. The only way to overcome this heredity which is the betrayal that came down through centuries is stand together.

You can also overcome by reconciliation of one another. This betrayal is the cool breeze that began to blow throughout the black families during their bondage in this country. Of course this might be hard for you to believe but it is true. You got to believe it not because it is being told you to.

Just do some research and have an open mind to accept the truth. This is not an idea that I had. This is facts. You do not hate each other or anyone. It was the despair hanging over your very souls and the obstacles that were in your way caused the betrayal.

Love and respect conquers in every nation, family and friend. We are not only supposed to love each other but every human being that is in the entire world. It does not matter what race or nationality. We have to love and forgive them.

One cannot give advice unless one has experienced the whole category that is spoken of. Whatsoever come upon an individual, they are fully the blame for it. One has to witness against oneself. Anyone can come out of an undesirable situation even if the situation was forced. You have been forced into many of things in this country whilst you were in slavery.

There is nothing that cannot be overcome in the darkest moment of life. No matter, it is a bright day today. Brighter days ahead are coming if God is willing. Our journey ahead is going to be easy. There will not be a struggle of survival; treading the water trying to keep the head emerged above for drowning. History is the past tense.

Today is present tense. Every black man, woman, boy and girl is free and equal today in this present tense. We are not in solitary anymore.

As I grew up I was always with a heavy heart filled with despair. Every black soul had the same despair. History did teach us about the slavery of yesterday.

History does not tell any lies about the slavery. It is all written. It cannot be undone. If there is any "die hard" amongst us today. I am sorry that you feel the way that you do. I feel sorry for you. It was very grieving to read of the inhumane, heartless condition that the black slaves of centuries ago underwent here in America.

Through trials and tribulations the old slaves pressed on. They reached their goals that we black people can look and see (I am speaking of the black historians). We black people should follow his or her footsteps. The slaves of yesterday paved the way for we black people today. Even though the slaves came from another country, this gave them the strength to press on hoping that they one day will finally be set free.

No one is complaining, wishing or willing themselves out of their life which Christ has given to them due to the hard time they have had. With the intention of it is not what one must do. If anyone has a pain in their body and knowing that the pain is there. The only remedy is just getting rid of the pain. There are remedies that will not destroy the body in doing so. Why complain about it. You knew that you were enslaved, but not anymore.

This is changing the thought somewhat momentarily but everyone is aware of their thoughts and actions. It would be a very hard thing to erase or dismiss the mind. Everything takes place in the heart and mind. Whatsoever the circumstance, the mind has thought upon it before it is willed: then action takes place it is view by the mind beforehand.

Peoples cannot go and commit a crime and cry out for mercy. Their cry is always the same they did not know what they were doing at the time. The mind had thought upon the crime beforehand it was willed in the heart.

The thoughts and actions brought it into a reality. This is the way that so many have won their freedom in the court room of justice. They pleaded the insanity deception. The mind does not get sick. Take for instance a child that is born with a mental disorder. That child can be taught and does understand.

Children, which are at birth deaf, mute, and blind, can be taught. So if the brain at birth is sound and healthy, it does not later on or throughout life become ill or become insane. Even cancer in the brain does not have any thing to do with the mind. The worst scenario of cancer is that it will take hold on any part of the body. Inside or out there is no part that cancer cannot take hold on.

Cancer will kill the entire body. It is very important that one consider their mind. Everyone is responsible for their minds. No one is accountable for anyone's mind but their own.

Just like in the past, there never were as many autistic children as of today. Can anyone prove that the Ultra Sound that is given today of the unborn fetes is not the reason for the outburst of autistics? Scientists say that this Ultra Sound is safe. They started experimenting with this device in the eighteenth century. This does not prove this Ultra Sound that scientists has discovery is safe to use on humans. Especially fetes that has not come forth into the light or air.

If the mind is fill with all matter of wickedness, evil and violence. The consequence will be paid. This is what the Caucasians did. They put it in their minds and hearts that the black race was not a part of humanity. They willed it and it became a reality with them. The mind cannot be killed. It goes on into deep sleep and only Christ can awaken the mind from the sleep.

It is the action of the enemy. I am not speaking of the Caucasians or any nationality as being our enemy. It is the wicked one; man's worst enemy and nightmare. He is humanity's enemy. He have come in and taken many souls captured by his own will.

It was not right when the Caucasian race went into the country of Africa and forced the African people to America, and then put them into slavery. No one is supposed to take that which does not belong to them. God created all men equal in the entire world. We black people of today have overcome by the help of Christ and by the courage of the black historians. Black slaves of centuries ago walked by faith not by sight.

We have today the contributions that the great black historian slaves contributed to humanity. Their contributions are being used by many nations. The determinations of the black slaves was strong. They went through the trials and tribulations of the Caucasians slavery here in America. They did not look around because they knew their conditions. It would not have given them any hope because there was not anyway for them to escape.

The great historians have passed on into history. Their records are here today for everyone to see. In the beginning of slavery here in the

United States of America for the black people sweat, blood, and life were drained from them. Not decades ago, not an isolated incident but centuries of slavery up until 2009. Who can describe their agony and defeat?

WORKS CITED

Booker, Bobby. "Hip-Hop's Leaders Address Negative Images of Women." The *Sunday Tribune* 22 Apr. 2007. Vol. 4, No. 23. Pg 4C.

Charlton, Angela. "France to Compensate Nuclear Test Victims." *Yahoo.com.* 22 Mar. 2009 <*http://news.yahoo.com/s/ap/20090324/ap_on_re_eu/eu_france_nuclear_...* >

Johnson, Tyree. "Jackson: We're Free, But Not Equal, Yet." *Westside Weekly* 29 Feb-7 Mar 2008. Vol. 20, No. 01. Pg 1.

Massie, Mychal. "America Has Apologized." NationalCenter.org, Project 21 Aug. 2003. <http://www.nationalcenter.org/P21NVMassieApology803.html>

McElrath, Jessica. About.com: African American History (Various Articles) 26 Jan-20 Apr. 2009. *About.com* 2009, a part of The New York Times Company.

Thompson, Garland. "The Crisis of Blacks in the U.S." *The Sunday Tribune* 22 Apr 2007. Vol. 4, No 23. Pg. 3C.